Quilting Designs for Sashing, Blocks...

Contents

How to Use the Patterns 2

Sashing, Block and Border Designs

Twist & Turn Daffodils – 2¼" 3	Carla's Conch – 2¾" 15
Window Boxes (Daffodil block – 4") 3	Carla's Conch – 1¾" 15
Betty's Twist & Turn – 1¾" 4	Carla's Conch Variations 16
Penelope's Plumes – 7¼" 5	Carla's Corner Variations 17
Penelope's Plumes – 4" 7	Overlapping Cirtcles – 3" 18
Stella's Delight – 4" 7	Circle Silhouette – 4" 18
Pumpkin Seed – 2½" 7	Overlapping Oval Corner – 2¼" 19
Caroline's Lattice – 3½" 8	Oval Silhouette – 3" 19
Caroline's Lattice – 2¼" 8	Viola's Vine – 3½" 20
Elba's Star Flowers – 3¾" 9	Doug's Design – 4" 22
Green's Garden – 2¾" 9	Laura's Cable – 2½" 24
Frank's Flower – 4½" 10	Little Angel – 7" 26
Frank's Flower – 2¼" 10	Cupid's Wings – 7" 27
Angela's Ribbon – 3¾" 11	Princess Sasa – 6" 28
Angela's Ribbon – 1½" 11	Donald's Kingdom – 6¾" 29
Elisa's Posies and Grid – 3½" 12	Cloud Nine Continuous – 9" 30
Bab's Berries – 1½" 13	Cloud Nine Traditional 31
Aimee's Chain – 1½" 13	Cloud Nine Appliqué Variation 31
Double Feather – 3¾" 13	Cloud Nine Sashing – 2½" 31
Daphne's Laurel – 3¾" 14	

©2013, from *Helen's Copy & Use Quilting Patterns* (AQS, 2002)

How to Use the Patterns

Over 30 patterns plus placement diagrams and reversed designs in a variety of sizes are presented in this book. An enlargement chart for 3" designs is on page 19 and for 7" designs is on page 26.

There's lots of overlap among the designs. Portions of block designs can be adapted for borders and vice versa; sashing designs can be repeated for borders; and so on. There are some continuous line motifs and design. All the designs can be enlarged or reduced and are approptiate for both hand and machine quilting.

I am known for folding patterns into perfect miters. I use the same trial-and-error steps to develop all of my repetitive pattern designs. Here is how it's done.

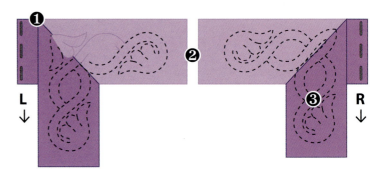

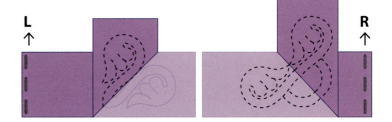

❑ Layer two copies facing together. Staple patterns at either end, then fold where you like the design. At least four different versions are always possible.

❑ Select the design you want and redraw an accurate copy.

❑ Make three or more copies, positioning this new design in borders, sashing, or block areas. Enlarge or reduce to fit the area to be quilted.

❑ For pre-planning, there are three places to begin positioning the quilting design: ❶ in the corner, ❷ in the center, or ❸ midway between, such as swags.

❑ You need three copies of the design and one of them should be the reversed image. They may not all be used, but having them gives you more choices.

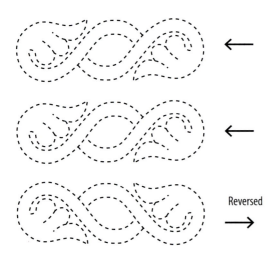

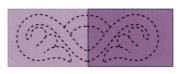 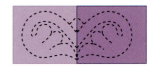

❑ Center reversals are easy to fold and can be adapted to fit any border or block measurement.

❑ Refer to pages 17, 22 and 24 for other step-by-step examples of how to use the patterns.

QUILTING DESIGNS *for* SASHING, BLOCKS & BORDERS — Helen Squire

Sashing, Block and Border Designs

■ Sashing

- ❏ A strip of fabric used to set pieced or appliquéd blocks together is called sashing.
- ❏ If cut 3" wide, it will measure 2½" finished. The direction the seams are pressed (toward the block or under the sashing strips) determines the size of the width to be quilted.
- ❏ Outline quilting is done ¼" away from the seams. In-the-ditch quilting is done on the side with no seam allowances underneath.

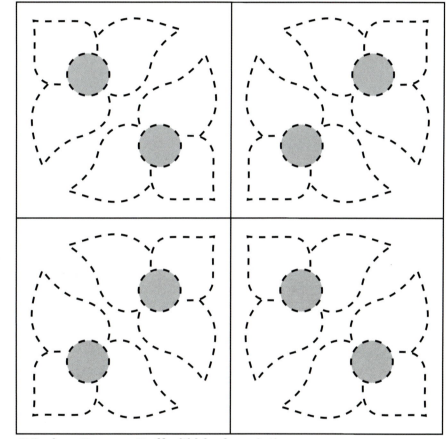

Window Boxes – Daffodil block variation

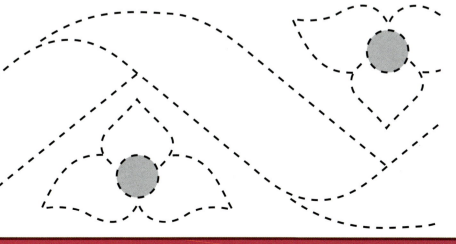

Twist & Turn Daffodils 2¼"

Sashing, Block and Border Designs

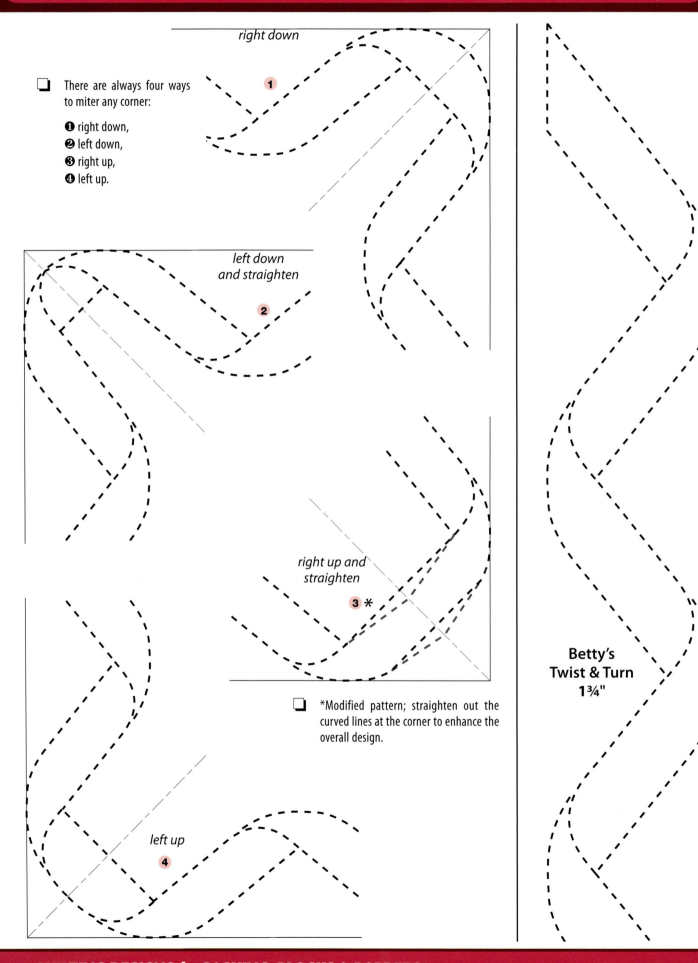

❏ There are always four ways to miter any corner:
- ❶ right down,
- ❷ left down,
- ❸ right up,
- ❹ left up.

right down

left down and straighten

right up and straighten

❏ *Modified pattern; straighten out the curved lines at the corner to enhance the overall design.

left up

Betty's Twist & Turn 1¾"

Penelope's Plumes
7¼"

Penelope's Plumes 4"

Placement Diagram

Sashing

QUILTING DESIGNS *for* SASHING, BLOCKS & BORDERS — Helen Squire

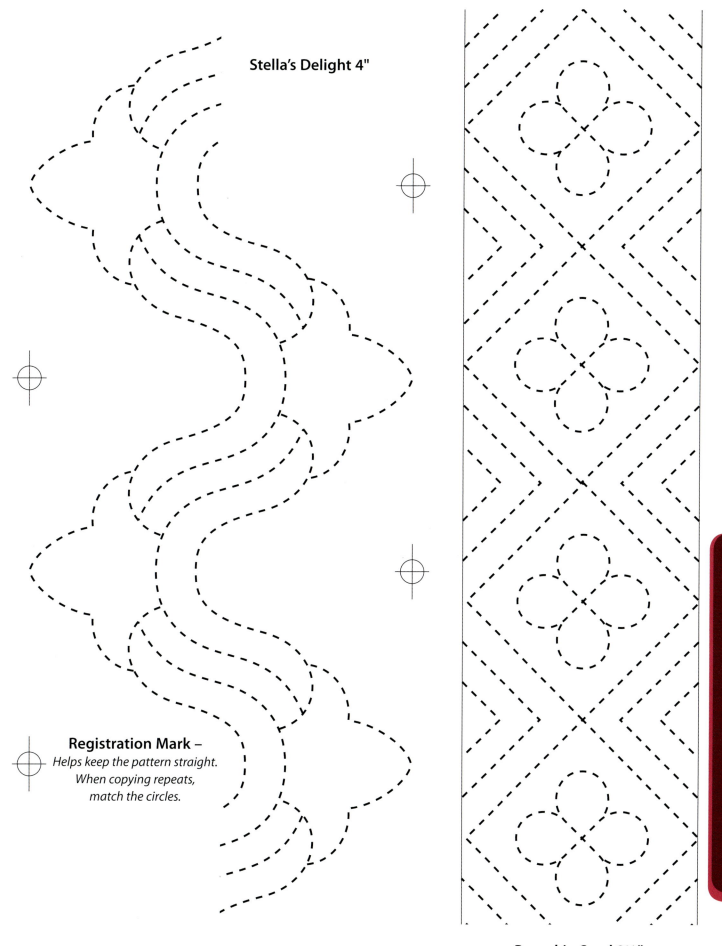

Stella's Delight 4"

Registration Mark –
Helps keep the pattern straight. When copying repeats, match the circles.

Pumpkin Seed 2½"

Caroline's Lattice 3½"

Caroline's Lattice 2¼"

Sashing

Elba's Star Flowers
3¾"

Green's Garden
2¾"

Placement Diagram

Frank's Flower
4½"

2¼"

Sashing

10   QUILTING DESIGNS *for* SASHING, BLOCKS & BORDERS   Helen Squire

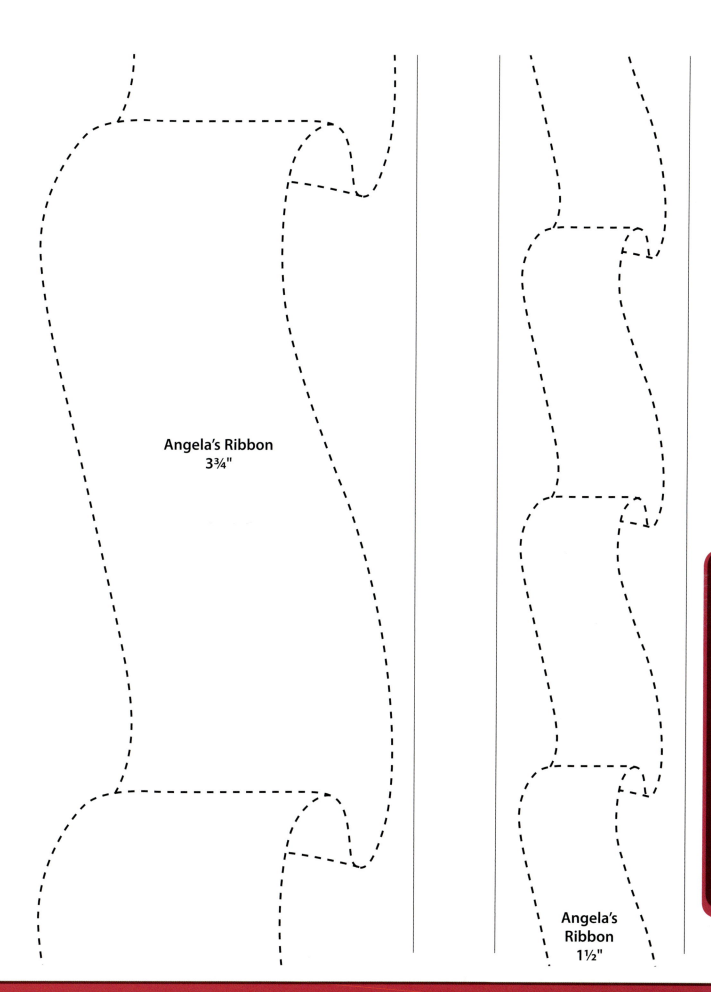

Sashing

Elisa's Posies and Grid 3½"

Placement Diagram

Bab's Berries
1½"

Aimee's Chain
1½"

Double Feather
3¾"

Sashing

QUILTING DESIGNS for SASHING, BLOCKS & BORDERS — Helen Squire

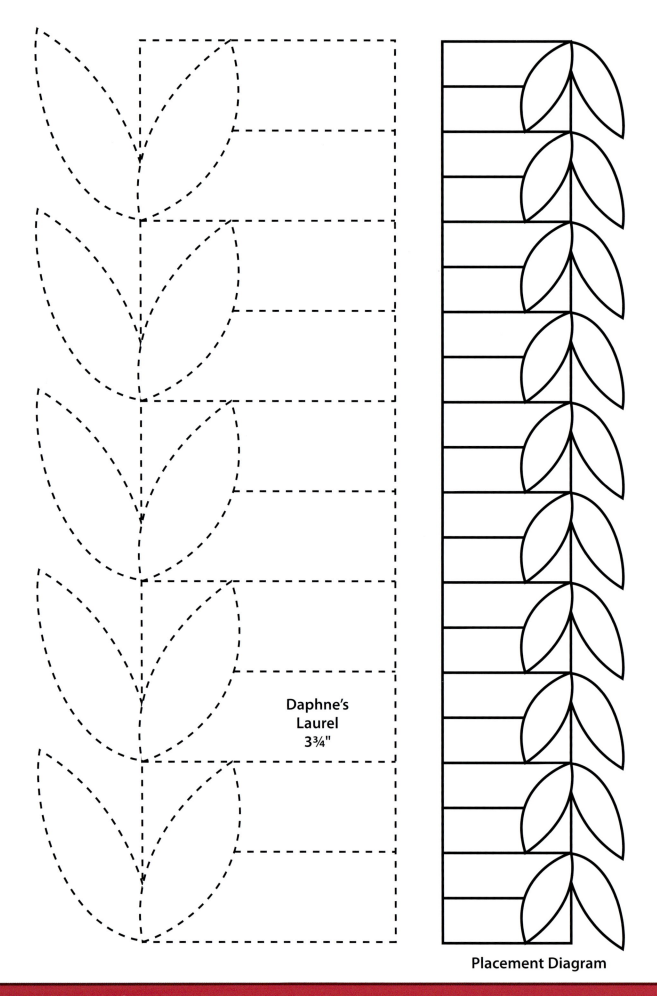

Daphne's Laurel 3¾"

Placement Diagram

Sashing

14 QUILTING DESIGNS *for* SASHING, BLOCKS & BORDERS — Helen Squire

Carla's Conch 2¾"   Carla's Conch 1¾"   Carla's Conch Reversed

Borders and Blocks

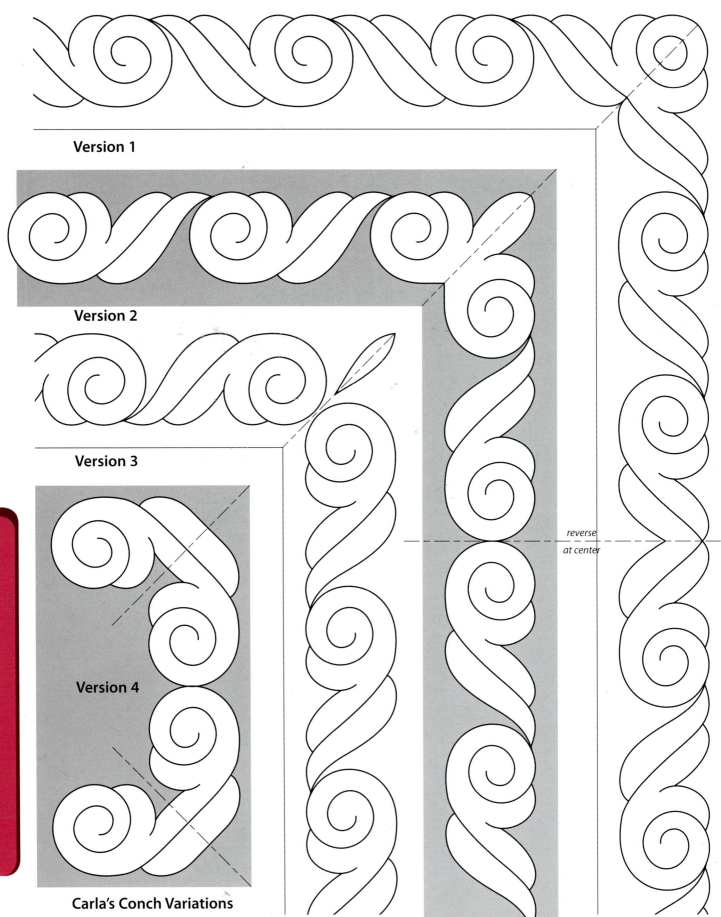

Version 1

Version 2

Version 3

Version 4

Carla's Conch Variations

reverse at center

Borders and Blocks

16 QUILTING DESIGNS *for* SASHING, BLOCKS & BORDERS Helen Squire

Pattern can be enlarged to any size

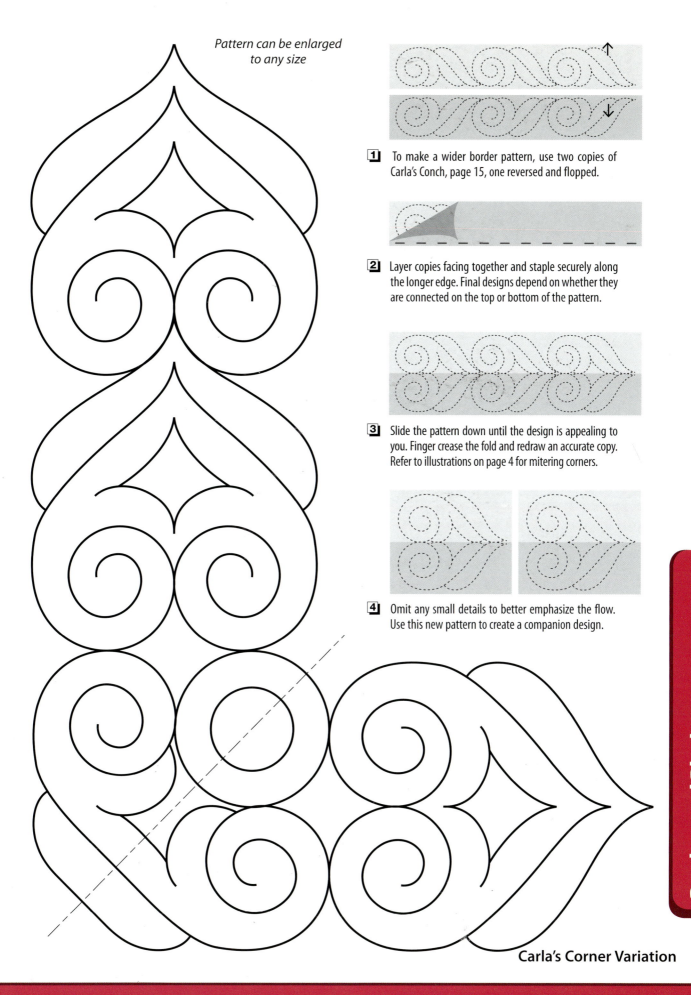

1. To make a wider border pattern, use two copies of Carla's Conch, page 15, one reversed and flopped.

2. Layer copies facing together and staple securely along the longer edge. Final designs depend on whether they are connected on the top or bottom of the pattern.

3. Slide the pattern down until the design is appealing to you. Finger crease the fold and redraw an accurate copy. Refer to illustrations on page 4 for mitering corners.

4. Omit any small details to better emphasize the flow. Use this new pattern to create a companion design.

Carla's Corner Variation

Borders and Blocks

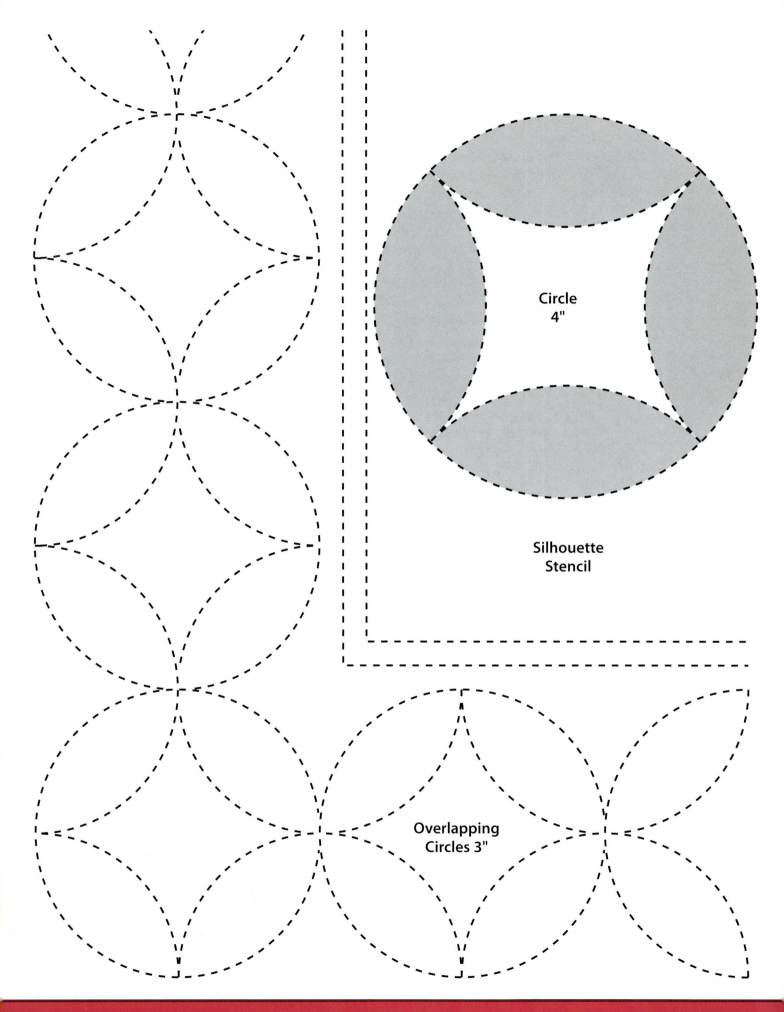

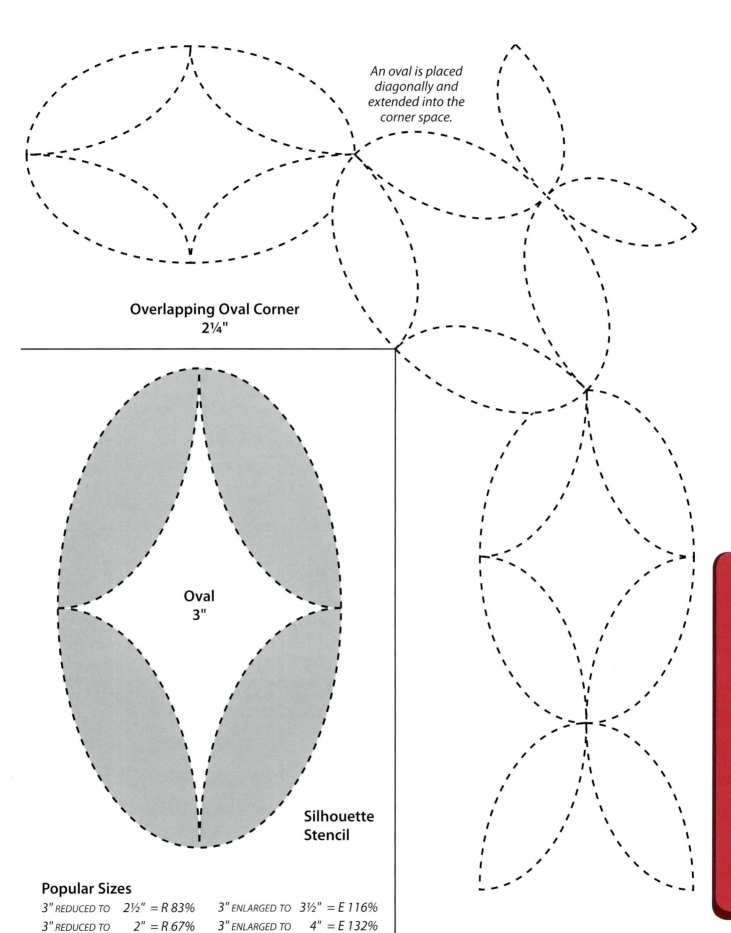

An oval is placed diagonally and extended into the corner space.

Overlapping Oval Corner
2¼"

Oval
3"

Silhouette Stencil

Popular Sizes

3" REDUCED TO	2½" = R 83%	3" ENLARGED TO	3½" = E 116%
3" REDUCED TO	2" = R 67%	3" ENLARGED TO	4" = E 132%

Borders and Blocks

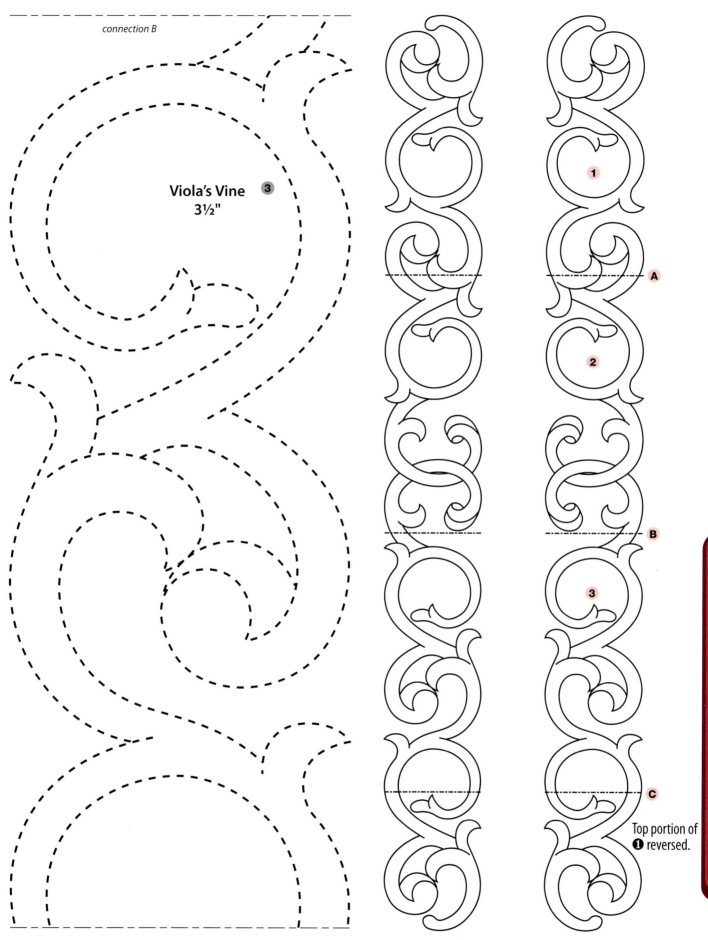

connection B

Viola's Vine ③
3½"

Placement Diagram

Top portion of ❶ reversed.

Borders and Blocks

QUILTING DESIGNS *for* SASHING, BLOCKS & BORDERS — Helen Squire

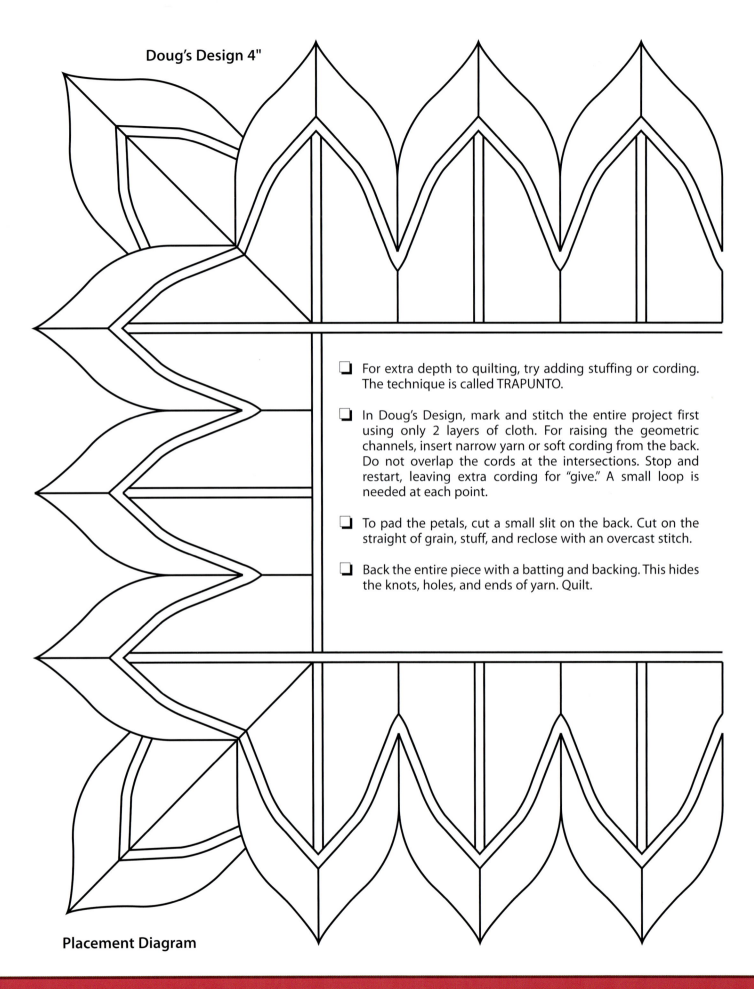

Doug's Design 4"

- For extra depth to quilting, try adding stuffing or cording. The technique is called TRAPUNTO.

- In Doug's Design, mark and stitch the entire project first using only 2 layers of cloth. For raising the geometric channels, insert narrow yarn or soft cording from the back. Do not overlap the cords at the intersections. Stop and restart, leaving extra cording for "give." A small loop is needed at each point.

- To pad the petals, cut a small slit on the back. Cut on the straight of grain, stuff, and reclose with an overcast stitch.

- Back the entire piece with a batting and backing. This hides the knots, holes, and ends of yarn. Quilt.

Placement Diagram

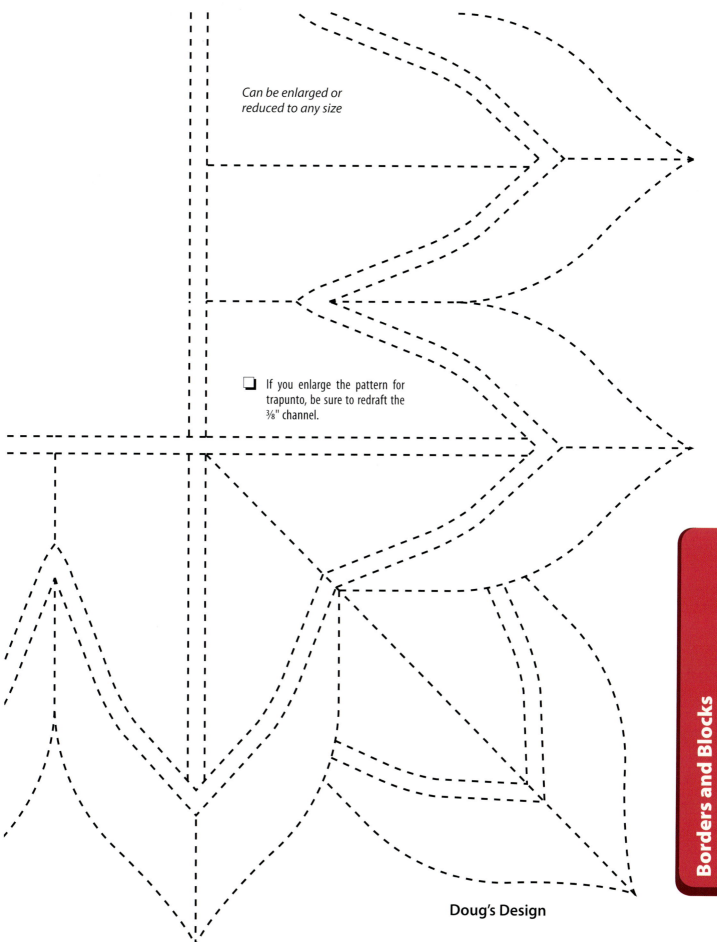

Doug's Design

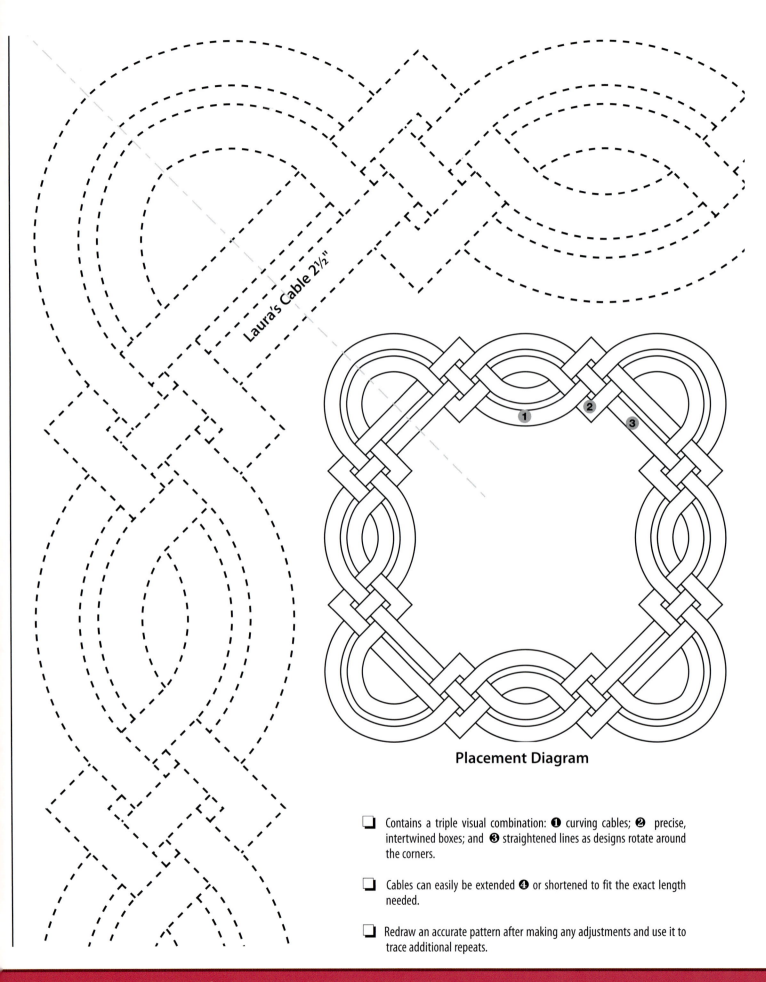

Placement Diagram

- Contains a triple visual combination: ❶ curving cables; ❷ precise, intertwined boxes; and ❸ straightened lines as designs rotate around the corners.

- Cables can easily be extended ❹ or shortened to fit the exact length needed.

- Redraw an accurate pattern after making any adjustments and use it to trace additional repeats.

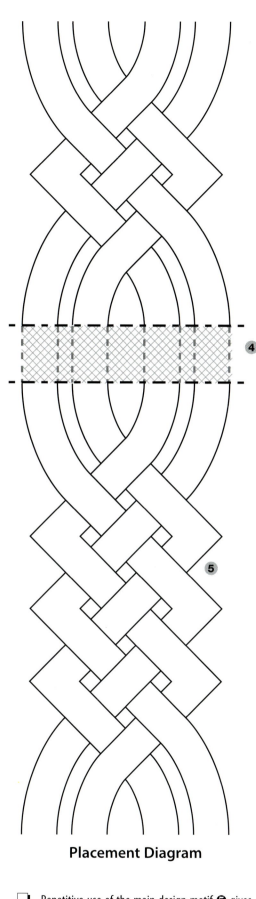

Placement Diagram

☐ Repetitive use of the main design motif ❺ gives extra emphasis.

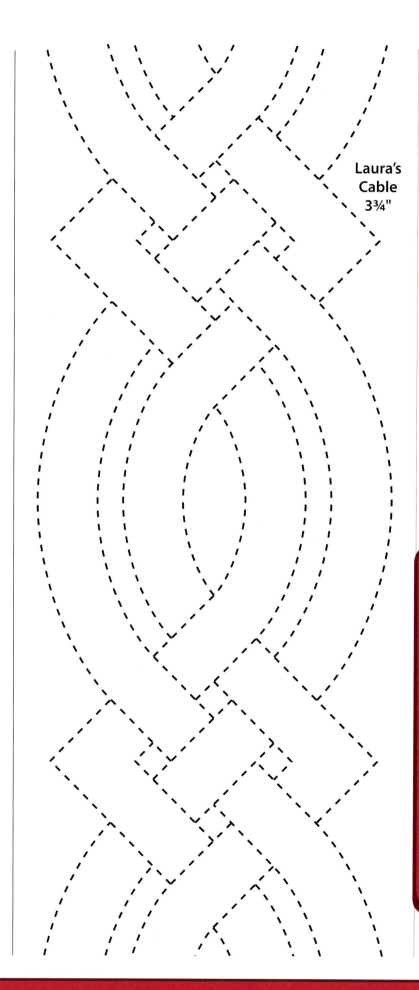

Laura's Cable
3¾"

QUILTING DESIGNS *for* SASHING, BLOCKS & BORDERS

Placement Diagram: Little Angel

Cupid's Wings 7"

Borders and Blocks

QUILTING DESIGNS for SASHING, BLOCKS & BORDERS — Helen Squire

Placement Diagram: *Alternate placement of the repeat creates entirely different looks.*

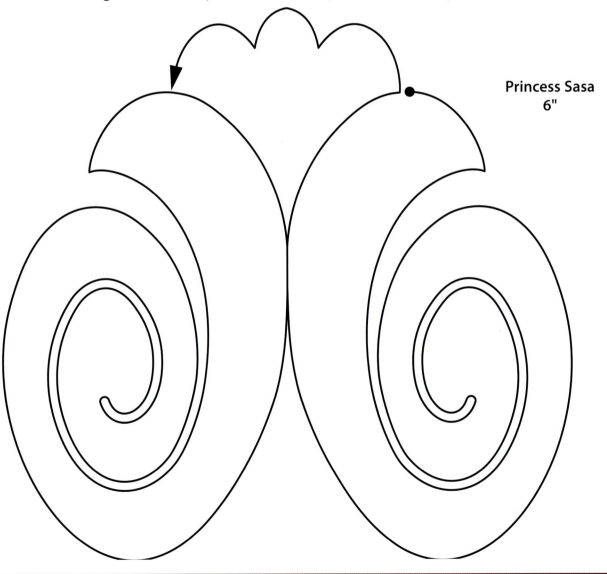

Princess Sasa
6"

Donald's Kingdom

▲ Placement Diagrams ▼

QUILTING DESIGNS for SASHING, BLOCKS & BORDERS — Helen Squire — 29

Cloud Nine Continuous
9"

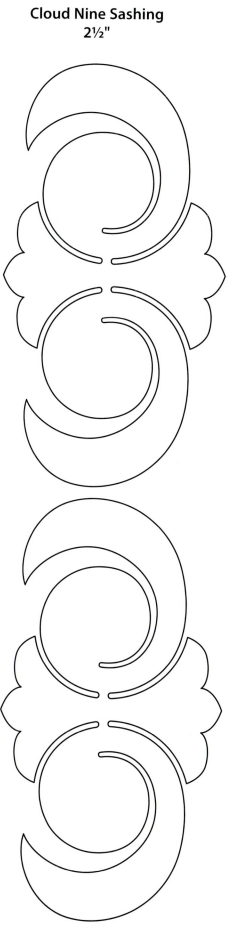

Cloud Nine Sashing
2½"

Cloud Nine Traditional

Cloud Nine Appliqué Variation

More AQS Books

This is only a small selection of the books available from the American Quilter's Society. AQS books are known worldwide for timely topics, clear writing, beautiful color photos, and accurate illustrations and patterns. The following books are available from your local bookseller, quilt shop, or public library.

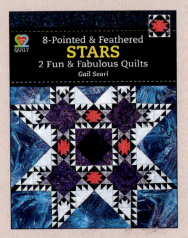
#1284

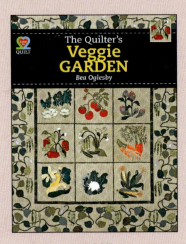
#1287

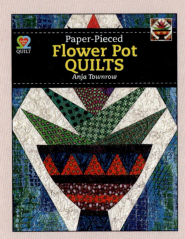
#1288

#1292

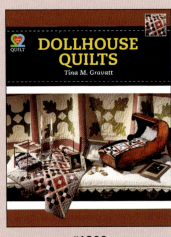
#1290

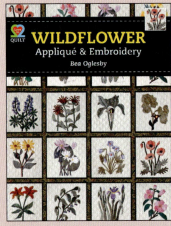
#1289

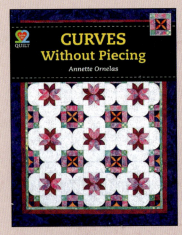
#1293

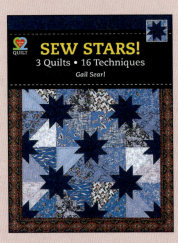
#1295

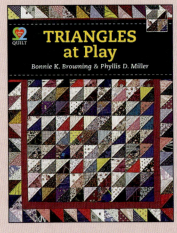
#1297

LOOK for these books nationally.
CALL or **VISIT** our website at

1-800-626-5420
www.AmericanQuilter.com